WITHDRAWN

South Carolina
The Palmetto State

Jason Glaser

PowerKiDS press.

New York

To Jean and Andy who, along with bringing back much helpful information about South Carolina from their trip, also happened to get married there

Published in 2010 by The Rosen Publishing Group, Inc.
29 East 21st Street, New York, NY 10010

First Edition

Editor: Amelie von Zumbusch
Book Design: Greg Tucker
Photo Researcher: Jessica Gerweck

Photo Credits: Cover © Bob Krist/Corbis; p. 5 © Eric Horan/age fotostock; pp. 7, 9 MPI/Getty Images; p. 11 Gary Randall/Getty Images; pp. 13, 22 (animal), 22 (flag), 22 (bird) Shutterstock.com; p. 15 Jerry Markland/Getty Images for NASCAR; p. 17 © www.iStockphoto.com/Rob Belknap; p. 19 Doris De Witt/Getty Images; p. 22 (tree) © www.iStockphoto.com/David Birkbeck; p. 22 (flower) JTB Photo/age fotostock; p. 22 (Andrew Jackson) Stock Montage/Getty Images; p. 22 (Marian Wright Edelman) Evan Agostini/Getty Images; p. 22 (Kevin Garnett) Jim Rogash/Getty Images.

Library of Congress Cataloging-in-Publication Data

Glaser, Jason.
  South Carolina : the Palmetto State / Jason Glaser. — 1st ed.
     p. cm. — (Our amazing states)
  Includes index.
  ISBN 978-1-4358-9345-0 (library binding) — ISBN 978-1-4358-9778-6 (pbk.) —
  ISBN 978-1-4358-9779-3 (6-pack)
  1. South Carolina—Juvenile literature. I. Title.
  F269.3.G56 2010
  975.7—dc22
                                          2009026803

Manufactured in the United States of America

CPSIA Compliance Information: Batch #WW10PK: For Further Information contact Rosen Publishing, New York, New York at 1-800-237-9932

Contents

Entryway to America

In many ways, South Carolina's Sea Islands show the **tough** character of the state. Mighty forces wanting to reach the land beyond the islands have had to get past them first. The Sea Islands serve as a **barrier** against powerful storms. Spain, France, and England all sailed through them to claim parts of North America for themselves. War ships and **pirate** ships have both battled off the Sea Islands' coasts.

South Carolina was one of the 13 **colonies** that broke away from Great Britain to form the United States. Today, South Carolina is part of the eastern United States along the Atlantic Ocean. North Carolina lies north of it, and Georgia sits along the state's west and south sides.

Today, many of South Carolina's Sea Islands are well-liked vacation spots. Hilton Head Island, seen here, is known for its golf courses, beaches, and natural beauty.

A Hard Beginning

Controlling South Carolina has never been easy. Spain and France fought over the land with each other and with the Native Americans living there. Later, Great Britain claimed the land and founded a colony, called Carolina.

Carolina's leaders had trouble keeping the southern part of the colony safe. Therefore, the British broke it into two colonies, South Carolina and North Carolina, in 1719. In time, the people of South Carolina and other colonies wanted to rule themselves. They fought for their freedom in the American Revolution. During the war, more key battles were fought in South Carolina than anywhere else. After the war, South Carolina became the United States' eighth state on May 23, 1788.

Here, South Carolina hero Daniel Morgan and other Americans are fighting in the Battle of Cowpens. This battle took place on January 17, 1781, in Cowpens, South Carolina.

Fighting for Rights

In the 1800s, South Carolina sold crops, such as cotton, rice, and **tobacco**, to many countries. These crops were often grown by African-American **slaves**. However, some Northern states wanted to outlaw having slaves. The U.S. government placed heavy taxes on goods from other countries, too. South Carolinians feared for their businesses.

Several Southern states wanted to leave the United States, as the colonies had left England. In 1861, South Carolina broke away from the United States. Other Southern states soon followed. This caused the Civil War. The war was hard on South Carolina. Cities were burned and many people died. In 1865, the South lost the war.

The Civil War started in Charleston, South Carolina, on April 12, 1861. Southern soldiers began firing on Union soldiers in Fort Sumter. Two days later, the Southerners took over the fort.

Wet and Warm

Being near the ocean means wet weather. The part of South Carolina that lies near sea level, called the Lowcountry, is warm year-round. Water pools up as **swamps**. Summers are hot, with lots of rain. Farther west, the air is drier and the land rises into sandy hills. Beyond that lies the Piedmont, or the flat land at the bottom of the mountains. The Blue Ridge Mountains are in the state's northwest corner. They are the state's highest part, rising up to 3,500 feet (1,067 m) high. The mountains keep South Carolina warm by blocking cold winds from the north.

Sometimes South Carolina is hit by storms called **hurricanes**. In 1989, Hurricane Hugo destroyed buildings across South Carolina with water and winds.

The swamps of South Carolina's Lowcountry are full of interesting and beautiful plants, such as the cypresses and water lilies seen here.

Life Near the Rivers and Trees

South Carolina is home to many things. Small, noisy Carolina wrens are found across the state. Alligators, lizards, and snakes creep through the river grasses. The state reptile, the loggerhead turtle, lays its eggs on the beaches. Opossums and red-tailed hawks rest in tall trees, such as the huge Angel Oak. This tree is over 1,400 years old!

The state tree, the palmetto, springs up on South Carolina's beaches. The walls of **Fort** Moultrie, on Sullivan's Island, South Carolina, were built from palmetto wood. During the American Revolution, 11 British ships fired **cannons** at the fort. The cannonballs stuck in the palmetto walls! Today, South Carolina calls itself the Palmetto State. Its people try to be as strong as palmettos.

Palmettos, such as the ones along this sidewalk, are a common sight in South Carolina. These trees are also known as sabal palms or cabbage palmettos.

Old Farms and New Businesses

South Carolina's **economy** has gone through some great changes. For hundreds of years, South Carolina's farm owners made money by growing and selling cotton, rice, and tobacco. They also raised a plant called indigo, which was used to make dye. Farmers today still sell these crops, but other businesses are also important. Some businesses make and sell things out of cotton. South Carolinians also build things people use every day, such as cars.

Today, a lot of money comes from visitors to the state. Travelers swimming at the beaches, playing golf, or visiting museums need places to eat and sleep. Visitors also spend money to watch horses or race cars speed around South Carolina's tracks.

These race car drivers have all won races at the Darlington Raceway, in Darlington, South Carolina. The track has drawn visitors to South Carolina for over 60 years.

Columbia

When most of South Carolina's colonists lived near the shore, Charleston served as the capital. Over time, though, many people began living farther away from the Lowcountry. Soon after the American Revolution, the capital moved to Columbia, which is nearer to the center of the state.

Today, Columbia is filled with a mix of new sights and old buildings that were rebuilt after being burned during the Civil War. The South Carolina State House has brass stars that mark where it was hit by cannonballs during that war. At the Riverbank Zoo, more than 2,000 animals run free in a modern park that does not use bars or cages. Instead, water, rocks, and lighting keep the animals and visitors apart.

The dome, or round roof, on top of the South Carolina State House is covered with 44,000 pounds (19,958 kg) of copper. The dome was added between 1900 and 1902.

The Well-Mannered City

When people talk about the **charm** of the South, they are often thinking about Charleston. Charleston is one of the oldest cities in the United States. Its people pride themselves on their friendliness and manners. The city's historic beauty makes it a top vacation spot.

Many visitors to Charleston buy sweetgrass baskets. The Gullah make these baskets by hand using grasses that grow on the nearby Sea Islands. The Gullah are **descendants** of West African slaves who lived on the Sea Islands.

Visitors to the city also walk through Battery Park. The park has great views of Sullivan's Island Lighthouse and Fort Sumter. Some people say the park is haunted by the spirits of dead pirates!

Many people visit Charleston to see the city's beautiful old buildings. Some visitors even travel around this historic city by horse and buggy.

Southern Cooking

One of the best things about South Carolina is its food. Anyone who lives there will tell you that South Carolina is the birthplace of **barbecue**. The wood from hickory trees gives the cooked meat its smoky taste. Plenty of mustard in the seasoning helps, too. Visitors to South Carolina can also eat crabs, shrimp, and oysters that were pulled fresh from the ocean.

While waiting for supper, you might want to snack on some boiled peanuts. You can buy these tasty treats from carts in parks and on city streets. A juicy peach might be nice, too. South Carolina grows more peaches than any other state except California. In South Carolina, you will never be bored or hungry!

Glossary

barbecue (BAHR-bih-kyoo) Food cooked outside on a grill, over an open fire, or over hot coals or wood.

barrier (BAR-ee-er) Something that blocks something else from passing.

cannons (KA-nuns) Large, heavy guns.

charm (CHAHRM) Ease at winning people's hearts.

colonies (KAH-luh-neez) New places where people move that are still ruled by the leaders of the country from which they came.

descendants (dih-SEN-dents) People who are born of a certain family or group.

economy (ih-KAH-nuh-mee) The way in which a country or state oversees its goods and services.

fort (FORT) A strong building or place that can be guarded against an enemy.

hurricanes (HUR-ih-kaynz) Storms with strong winds and heavy rain.

pirate (PY-rut) Having to do with people who attack and rob ships.

slaves (SLAYVZ) People who are "owned" by another person and forced to work for him or her.

swamps (SWOMPS) Wet land with a lot of trees and bushes.

tobacco (tuh-BA-koh) A plant used for smoking or other uses.

tough (TUF) Strong or firm.

South Carolina State Symbols

**State Tree
Palmetto**

**State Animal
White-Tailed
Deer**

State Flag

**State Bird
Carolina Wren**

**State Flower
Yellow
Jessamine**

State Seal

Famous People from South Carolina

Andrew Jackson
(1767–1845)
Born in Waxhaws, SC
U.S. President

**Marian Wright
Edelman**
(1939–)
Born in Bennettsville, SC
Children's Rights Activist

Kevin Garnett
(1976–)
Born in Greenville, SC
Basketball Player

South Carolina State Map

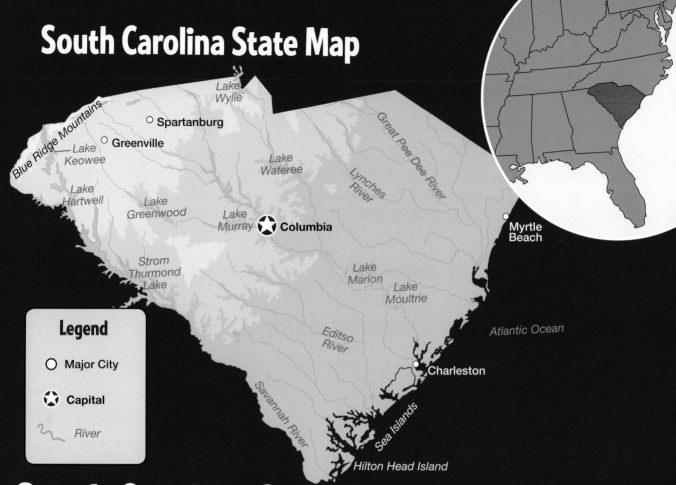

South Carolina State Facts

Population: About 4,012,012

Area: 31,113 square miles (80,582 sq km)

Mottoes: "Dum Spiro Spero" ("While I breathe, I hope") and "Animis Opibusque Parati" ("Prepared in mind and resources")

Songs: "Carolina," words by Henry Timrod and music by Anne Custis Burgess, and "South Carolina on My Mind," words and music by Hank Martin and Buzz Arledge

Index

Web Sites

Due to the changing nature of Internet links, PowerKids Press has developed an online list of Web sites related to the subject of this book. This site is updated regularly. Please use this link to access the list:
www.powerkidslinks.com/amst/sc/